Living Pendulums

B.S. Elaine Alli

WESTBOW
PRESS®
A DIVISION OF THOMAS NELSON
& ZONDERVAN

WestBow Press books may be ordered through booksellers or by contacting:

WestBow Press
A Division of Thomas Nelson & Zondervan
1663 Liberty Drive
Bloomington, IN 47403
www.westbowpress.com
1 (866) 928-1240

ISBN: 978-1-5127-4115-5 (sc)
ISBN: 978-1-5127-4116-2 (e)

Print information available on the last page.

WestBow Press rev. date: 10/13/2016

Contents

About the Author

Bibi Saphora Elaine Alli, well known far and wide as Elaine Alli, was born in December 1935 to a humble home in Sparendaam Village on the Eastern Coast of the Demerara River in Guyana. After obtaining a full primary education, she wrote the Pupil-Teacher's Examination (an entrance into the teaching profession) with ambitions of becoming a trained teacher. However, fate decreed she be an ordinary housewife; her father arranged a marriage and she got married at seventeen. She is the mother of eight children — three girls and five boys, one boy died. Her husband was ten years older than she was, but he was also a quiet, mild-tempered man and thus, her marriage survived.

Elaine is a voracious reader and so she gained her knowledge; she was often found in the late stages of a pregnancy falling asleep with a book in one hand and a dictionary in the other. In addition, she is also a deep lover of nature and it is from this that she draws her poetic inspiration.

Thoughts In A Cemetery

Here below
In this abandoned cemetery
Amidst dust and bones
Lie buried
Corrupted human lust, greed, lies, deceit
All cravings for earthly wealth
All — from sod to sod dissolved

Not only these
For Life
is a mixture of good and bad.

Here below
Lies buried love
Fulfilled and unfulfilled
Honest sweat for survival
Once in a struggling world above
All — into nothingness vanished.

Here below
Lies buried
Nations against nations feud for power
Some lost — some won
All conquered by death
And tramped by man and beast.

Here below
Lie buried
Many secrets, concealed eternally
In the heart of their Origin Mother
and lost with Time.

Here below
Lie buried
Struggles for human rights
Against human injustices
All from dust — to dust
In time
When turned by spade
Will by the breezes blow
And to the atmosphere lost.

Here above
I see a tall cross,
Lower, an epitaph
Its inscription
The Identity of
A Bishop's flight
On wings of fire
to eternal life.

Here above
I see not far away
Another
The identity of a child
Bourne on the bier of drowning
To the unknown realm
On my left
A mother in oblivion lost
Whilst in travail
Along the paths of childbirth.

Looking around I see
Closely matted grass
Obscuring many unknown.

Thoughts, thoughts
Turbulent thoughts
Are life's struggles, cares, thrift
self denial, victories and power
Worth their cause?
For when all be gone
Time be ceased
And memory no more
What would be left?

Living Pendulums

They open at night
And close with day.
Like white stars
In green skies.
They do not sparkle;
but smile.
The skies are
like velvet beds of green
With ornaments set.
Ornaments —
yet not artificial;
They are living gems.
I have not to look up
but
From my window
I look down.
Though below;
Their beauty is unsurpassed.
A fortnight ago
they were stars.
To-day — yard-long squashes.
Like green pendulum breasts
Luscious and heavy
Dangling from green cows
Ready for milking.
To-day — I admire.

To-morrow
I shall garner.
The next day
sell.

At bloom next crop time
Come
Gaze with me
Then
Patiently watch day by day
That you too be inspired
And
Composed verses
So the beauty of the squash vine
Be written
On the pages of Time.

Nature's Kins

Chanticleer!
You faithful heralder of the dawn
Ever obedient
To your 'Sovereign's' mandate
Your clarion echoes.
Mighty Phoebus
Majestic 'Monarch Of The Day'
Slowly rises
And takes possession of the sceptre
From
Silver-bonded 'Miss Lunar'
Princess of the night.

Gently rising
His golden staff, he reaches forth
And
Touches that opaque arch above
Gradually, transforming
This canopy of blue
Into a kaleidoscope of resplendence
Purple, golden — glinted oranges
And crimson.

Now earthwards
He gently sheds his golden rays
And behold!
All creation is gilted

Flowers and plants
From dreamland their exit smile
Whilst
The birds chirp out an anthem
As on their wings they rise
To greet the 'Master Of All Light'
Look!
His spell he casts
and glistening pearls
Of splendour great
The dew transform.

Oh! Mother Nature
What magnificent Offsprings
You have bourne
To-day
Their moods, all coincide
See — 'Lady Breeze' fuel of life,
Gently creation she caresses
And softly rocks the trees
Whilst a building melody she hums
Mighty Atlantic, 'King Of Waters'
How gently he undulates
To-day
Smoothly blends all kins of royalty.

Oh! Mother Nature
See — your royal offsprings
How they in their majestic trance
Enrapt
A slowly wakening universe.

Benediction

Withering, dying
Pantering, sweltering
In an immature hell
Were all of life of earthly sustenance
When
Like the flashes of a lighthouse
A life - savings signal to sailors at sea
So
The blinding flashes from the beacon of heaven
Are a signal of hope
To suffering man
In a sea of drought.

Dark and angry
Fearfully threatening
Angry because of their burden;
A burden becoming unbearable
Their threats though fearful
Are yet hopeful
Then
As if in accord with each other's mood
The heavens belched!
An ominous sound
It's deafening peals echoing
through the universe.

The 'Dark and Angry'
Showered sprays of sputum earthwards
Then retched and retched
Downpours of liquid vomit
Drenching (and parching) a parched
and crusty earth.
The earth, it's thirsty maw
Gulped and consumed
In ravenous gulps
The 'liquid of Life'.
All living vegetation
Revelling in their torrential bath.
Their shrivelling bodies consumed
with thirst.
First they sipped,
then swallowed the life-saving drops.
As they changed from drops
To tumultuous tides, raging from above.
The 'dark and angry',
The 'blinding flashes',
The belch of the heavens,
The deluge of liquid vomit.
All ominous.
Yet, a benediction
To a world in panic of drought.

My Bouquet

Of all the treasures of this earth
That to the soul brings mirth,
That freshens, and enlighten the swiftly passing hours,
Are the ever lovely flowers.

Lily of the velvet robe.
Crowned Queen of this pleasant globe
Thou art indeed the fairest flower
That e'er the sun had shone upon.

Of all the beauties man has seen,
None like unto the rose had been.
Words cannot describe the joy imparted
To many young and tender hearted.

By the fragrance of the sweetly scented rose
Which so tenderly grows
My heart doth vote for thee
Pretty blushing lady.

But of all those that lowly be
The hyacinth most appeals to me
Oh! Delicate flowers of hue so light
Thou was fashioned for my delight
With thy tender petals so blue
Which Mother Nature gave to thee,
Little hyacinth so free
I shall your lover ever be.

No other gift for Mother's Day
Is as pleasant as a frangipani bouquet
To the snowy-petalled Jasmine
This compliment I pay;
For both her beauty and perfume in bloom
Fill the air with fragrance when in bloom.

Greetings! To Princess of the radiant hour
Who arches gracefully the entrance to my bower.
Her name to know you need no guess
Bougainvillea of the crimson dress.

Jump-up and kiss-me, hibiscus, flamboyant and
immortelles
To them I'll give the honour as scarlet bells
And not forget the yellow warm-hearted
Sun-flower that keeps on smiling since the spring has
started

God's most careful plan
Everlasting joys of man
And Sunshine of my weary heart
My bouquet, God's works of art.

Life

What a golden dream is life,
T' is but a mixture of earthly strife
Seeing this just a cul-de-sac.

Oh! Brothers and sisters in humanity awaken
Let all thine opportunities best be taken,
Do ye not know? This life is but a test,
For eternity happy will all be the best.

Brothers and sisters for purpose all were create
To honour reverent and great
Adore the Almighty
Yes! Homage to him above the blue beyond
Too all creation that doth respond.

Oh! Master with us please do be
For weak without thine help will us all be
The eternal prize can no money buy
The rich, the poor and beggars for all laid by

In after life like the horizon be no end
So let us all our minds for prize millennium bend
Wealth or poverty our goal is but one
Therefore brothers and sisters the best must make
From now till death come on.

The Sea

Oh! Omnipotent most visible grandeur
Sorrow balm so my heart may endure
The tortures of life extreme strife
When riches and pains so engulf my life
To the profound beauty of the sea.

Friendship

Riches may be in stables
Beauty will decay
But true friendship will last
Till death drives it away.

Lovely Night

Oh! The glories of this tropic night
Enchanted by a silvery light
From the heavens blue above
Reflecting on a silent sea
My (heart) soul doth yearn with sudden love
For a life unfettered and free, magnificent sea
I, this lonely soul doth, wonder to enjoy the peace of
solemnity
Billowing waves come rolling in
As if to enshroud my soul within.

Hypnotic and entrancing doth thine majestic beauty be
The sea, the sea the wide and bottomless sea
So until eternity shall thine magical beauty ever be
Thou alone a proof that God Supreme exist,
Conqueror and ruler of a universe so confused and trust,
Thou a creation to joy enhance
To the race called humans
So easy to corrupt by least mischance.

Pain

I felt a pain, Oh! God
Know not any whom created from sod
Thou dweller of the chambers of mine heart
Problems and grief are so filled in every part.

How long or how much can I endure?
Oh! Please, my Master! Lead this sinner safe to your shore
Where sins, sorrows and pains are oblivion
This solution was my opinion.

But when I called, thou showed me hope
Before in darkness did I grope?
Brothers and sisters of human race
The cure of mind, soul
To him should we all embrace.

Carifesta

Dear islands of the Caribbean
Likened unto a constellation
From above when seen
They are the head and Guyana the tail
So pals Carifesta we hail.

Who could have guessed of such?
Many islands and races much
All blending in one family
United in co-operative friendships warmly.

That's something Carifesta approaching at a rapid rate
I've something to celebrate
Come brothers and sisters from far and wide,
With pleasure you are welcome inside.

Guyana! Oh Guyana!
Country of my birth,
Let's all join in gaiety and mirth.
Sons of the soil are us all.
So unite and never let us fall.
Carifesta! Carifesta! Make haste
and beckon to our call.

Untitled

In the wake of the planets circling
Night so long mine heart had sought;
Now holding me deeply wrap't in thought
With natural beauties plainly shown
Such as the yellow sands in the moonlight ambered
Ten years from now when I am grown
Will the sweetness of this moment be remembered?
Will these my childish dreams and plans
Come true within one decade of life spans?
O lovely night ! Thy beauties and my charms,
The glories are they of mine haven,
While happiness here I spend
Within my heart will be deeply engraven
Sweet memories to last until the end.

Faith

Oh! For hope the age — old food of mortal life
The all — providing fuel of sublime strife
Alas! When pains and sorrows desperate be,
And engulfed by all afflictions is humanity,
T'was the grasp of this same faith so fervent,
That saved us all from life so varied seas of failure and relent.
How often has sorrows black shadows fallen
Across life's ever winding paths to darken
So each forward step of men may be entangled.
But alas! For thou oh! Faith against must sorrows struggle,
His enemy most strong by God create,
Withdrawn most humbly conquered by faith.

Life's Dreams

What a golden dream is life,
T'is a tangle of varied earthly strife
Awaken and use must all humanity.

Specially For Rose Bud

In the dusky dusk of a fading twilight;
The gates of heaven open'd
And a blessing was downward cast;
For a star fell into my lap.
Suddenly the star transformed
Behold — — — — —
A beautiful vision before me laid
A tiny dew-drenched rose
Of a delicate hue so pink
In a garden fenced with cobalt blue
Was this a gimmick of my eyes
Or just another passing dream - I wondered.

The stars and moon
In all their glorious decorum of the skies
Cannot so much joy befill me
In this evening of my life
As that star and rose
That fell into my lap
For my darling "Michee"
The rose of unparalleled beauty
Was no other but Y O U.

Peacefully lying in your infantile repose
The Garden - - your bed - - the cobalt fence - -
Your crib's own slats.

"PRIDE OF MY HEART"
"JOY OF MY LIFE"
"SALVATION OF MY EYES"

Come
Rest your head upon Grandma's breast;
And dream thine "babehood days" away.

Mother's Love

Mother! Oh Mother! Your love is so strong;
No matter what crime, no matter what wrong
Your children no malice you bear
So many of them, yet equally your love you share.

Sorrows and pains derived from sin;
Most of all this world to bring them in;
Pains, discomfort for nine months all;
Yet yearns your heart for a babe's crying call.

"Tell me little ones, tell me truly",
Can anyone ever repay a mother fully?
NO..... this is impossible.
A mother's love how deep, how noble;
Throughout the world it is incomparable.

Fruits

Slender and stately be the stems
Gracefully carrying diadems.
Blended petals of flowers
Clustering forming corollas.

Bees keep buzz, buzz, a-buzzing.
Then brush, brush, a-brushing.
So the pollen goes a-rushing
Spreading tales of joy.
Oh! Ho! There ahoy!

We are coming through pistils
In the ovaries to fulfil
Mis-sions by commanding will.
Ovules mixing with pollen
For making fruits a-golden.
For tiny mouth a-watering.
Watering and a-waiting.
A-waiting for munching.

Raindrops

Pitter, Patter on my roof,
Like the clatter of a hoof,
Drip, drip, dropping all night long,
They keep singing this same song.

Their song they sing till morning come,
Then to the sun they say 'welcome',
Sunshine glistening drops so bright
Make me laugh with great delight.

The trees all bathe and drink,
Ponds and trenches flow to brink,
They keep pitter, patter all the day,
Then to the seas they flow away.

A Joy

Fresh little leaves so green
Hidden beneath unseen,
Butterflies bright and gay
As eggs they quietly lay.
How unsightly to see
These little eggs can be
When into worms they change,
Though, God did so arrange.
Caterpillars they spin
Cocoons in to begin
A me-ta-mor-phi-sis.
In time out will emerge
With colours brightly splurge
Beautiful, beautiful
BUTTERFLIES.

My Pet

My puppy white and brown
With spots upon your crown.
Who made your coat of hairs
And gave you paws in pairs?
Who gave you voice to bark
And chase the thieves at dark?
Who makes you frisk and run
And makes so much fun?
Who makes you chew my bone
And never me you leave alone?
It was God who made you
So alive and ever true
My puppy white and brown.

"A L U R E"

Eldorado city of gold
Martinez the teller told,
A Spaniard was set adrift
Then saved by Indians kind lift.
In a very small canoe
Like Winken-Blinken's little shoe,
To Guiana's shore they took him,
Night and day did him they look,
Until as he stronger grew
To gold and diamonds he drew.
Making a tale far-fetched,
Manoa City of Gold he dreamt,
Luring to explore with contempt
Many nations, far and wide
But *We* the winners Fate decide.
Dreamer myself I often wish
Juan's dream to be accomplish.

KIS — KA — DEE

Little Kis-ka-dee
Happy as can be.
On my fence you sit
Filling bit by bit
My small heart with glee
Kis, Kis-ka-dee.

With each song you sing
A message you bring
At birth of the day
"Come listen," you say
I listen to hear,
To all now I bear,
Kis, kis, kis-ka-dee
Come, listen and see,

Look at the flowers
These early hours.
Listen to the bees
All buzzing with ease,
Look at the trees
Now hear the breeze
Kis, kis, kis-ka-dee.

Flowers, bees, trees, breeze,
Together they make
A world, not a fake
Full of joy and fun
With rise of the sun
Kis, kis, kis-ka-dee.

The Sea

The big, big, sea
A man is he
With each his mood
He makes me brood.
When he is calm
He is a balm.
Then I wade
And also bathe
When he has froth
He is not wrath.
Then in him
I do, swim,
When he's storming
Thoughts keep forming
Shapes of fear
That makes me scare.
When he is muddy
He makes me study.
When he is clear
Then I can bear
A day of woe
As on I go.

My Country

I will tell you a story
of Guyana in geography.
Natural regions four.
Coastal belt by Atlantic Shore.
Sand and clay with lofty hills
Rivulets like singing rills.
The forest great, with trees
A-swaying in the breeze.
Ferns and shrubs profusely grow
With gold an diamonds below.

Great greasy plains
Striving with rains.
Like green tennis boards
Feed for cattle hoards.
Rivers three meandering
To the seas a-wandering
Essequibo be the tallest
With it's borders of green forest.

Also
Tiny doted islands
Their beaches lined with sands.
Demerara's "Garden City"
The Middle of this Trinity
Port Georgetown at its mouth
For east, west, north and south.
Berbice with New Amsterdam grand
Like Old Amsterdam of Holland.
Geography of our country
So interesting in poetry.

My Kite

I see you rising in the sky
And I think of Christ ascending high
I see the birds go sailing all away
And think of ships a-gliding in to bay.

I see the clouds a-floating
And think of kids a-boating.
I see the skies above us all
And think a roof most tall.
I feel my feet beneath all sore
And think the earth a hard, hard floor...

One big roof and floor
One big family core.
In one big house we link
Of all these I think
As here below I lay
A watching you this Easter Day.

Name Her

There is a lady on my shelf
Murmuring there all to herself.
Tick-tuck, tick-tuck, tick
I must be very quick.
When I look I see up there
When I listen I also hear.

The busiest hands that have ever been
the roundest face that ever seen.
Her hands they work the most
Yet she has never boast.
A face that all must look upon
Yet she seem to scorn no one.
She is one who talks so plenty.
Yet her brains are never empty.
Tick-tuck, tick-tuck she will say
As she hurries on her way.

Tamarind Tree

Little Tamarind tree
Wonder if I would see
Your trunk grow tall and fat
So beneath I may squat
And think of childhood days
And all my simple ways.

Happy to see cows graze
Or your spreading foliage
Growing big so big with age
Or, streams just running by
and birds above so high.
Little Tamarind tree
Wonder if I would see?
You as big as can be.

A Touch Of Beauty

There is always beauty
In the Almighty's handiwork
A moonlight night
A dark and starry night
A sunny day
A rainy day
Buds unfurling at morn
Sunlight kissing flowers
Leaves washed by rain
Grass damp and wet with dew.

There is always glory in Nature's sounds
The warbling of birds
The chirping of crickets
The pitter, patter of rain.

There is always joy in Nature's odour
The fragrance of the rose
The sweet scent of the jasmine
The perfume of the oleander
The freshly cut grass
A mango ripe and succulent
There is always beauty
There is is always beauty in all that
God has done.

Acknowledgements

First and foremost, my deepest appreciation, love and heart-felt gratitude to my eight children, who mean all the world to me – especially Sheik, who has worked tirelessly pursuing the publication of this book. To the late Ms. DeFlorimente, my school teacher, who recognized my potential at a young age and to the late A.J. Seymour, who encouraged me to continue writing. Nazia and Alia, my two granddaughters, thank you for your devotion to the publication of these poems. Finally, I owe everything to Suabi and Neville Ramnarain for making my dream of being a published poet come true. Thank you, everyone.

www.ingramcontent.com/pod-product-compliance
Lightning Source LLC
Chambersburg PA
CBHW030525290526
45786CB00004B/1623